GENEALOGY
QUICK TIPS FOR BEGINNERS

Tips From 25 Years Of Family Searching

Author

Kaye Nicholson

Collaborating With
Juanita Bowers Owens

ISBN-13: 978-1540382092
ISBN-10: 1540382095

DEDICATION

We dedicate this book to all the people searching for their ancestors.

This book is to help in your search of your family history. I've been working on my family history for over 25 years and do not claim to be an expert but a layman who has seen books mislead and some that confuse a beginner in genealogy.

When I began searching my family history, I had no one around to teach me the in's and out's of how it was done. I purchased many books but each gave a few pieces of information on searching out your ancestors. Some books don't go into detail about things you need to know or what you need to search for in your quest.

If you are a beginner, you must brace yourself for the overwhelming amount of information in libraries, courthouses record rooms and even the amount of things you find on the internet. Not all information is correct and you will find that some family members trees differ in names, dates, locations and even burials. It begins to get you down but don't ever let this slow you down.

I've helped people research their family histories over the years and I always tell them that sometimes information dribbles in and sometimes it slaps you in the face. Thinking on it now, it amuses me somewhat the way information has come to me. So I decided with the help of my best friend, Juanita Bowers Owens to reach out to the beginner genealogist and place our hands on your back and give some learning tips that can be found in books but mostly it is experience of researching our ancestors and trials and the errors that we want to help people avoid.

This book is not listed as Chapters but in Sections, I will also give a few examples in some sections to hopefully help you understand some of things you will find on your search.

SECTION ONE
TRANSPORTATION

Having a way to get to courthouses, libraries and graveyards is essential in doing research. Some try to do this from their home without going out and doing the work themselves. I worked a full time job and was taking care of my daughter but I always found a hour here or there to get out and do a few hours of research. I found this was more therapeutic for relieving stress and even walking through my family history in my mind. Juanita worked on her family history as time was allowed because of her job.

Some people don't live around where their ancestors grew up and lived but this should not stop you from researching. It is never good to depend on others to do the work for you, it can be helpful to have others that are researching to talk to but sometimes this is not an option.

When I would find a piece of information, I dragged my daughter many miles across the country in search of ancestors. What I realized after doing it for a while, she was learning the family history with me. This made it fun. Trust me, thinking about it now, she probably would have liked to slept in during her teenage years instead of standing in the middle of some cemetery in the cold and snow. I would even drag her friends with us and they became interested in their family histories, I'm glad that it was becoming important for them to learn of how their ancestors lived, worked and survived during the early years.

Don't limit your research to only the courthouses and libraries, please take advantage of the local historical societies in the area. Gather a list of phone numbers and addresses for future use to write letters or emails, some will help for free but don't take it personally if they want to charge for copying or research.

I began my search before cell phones were invented. I bought a decent digital camera when they first came out, Road Atlas and large box of sidewalk chalk and put it in my trunk. It is the pieces of equipment that was most important to me at the time but times have changed; many people now are post pictures of gravestones, personal pictures and so much information over the internet that I get my clues then do my research. So off we go, I hope you find these tips and suggestions helpful in your research.

Purchase or download a family history program. In the beginning, I tried to keep it all on paper and in notebooks but after a few months, I had to download a free program for my family tree.

Let me explain why, I would talk to someone about the family, I found myself going through papers and notebooks which cut into my time of finding out information. After meeting others who were researching, I discovered many new ways to do things.

Researching is a process, I was told to work on the family history one family at a time. I found this best until I got the hang of it. I discovered the volume of information had to be separated by family members.

The story always begins with YOU, then your parents and so on. It expands with each generation and soon you find yourself in a whole sea of family. I worked on one family member at a time, discovering every detail I could about that family member. It included their spouses, children, grandchildren and any military or accomplishments they had. Each family member becomes a story in itself.

SECTION TWO
PIECING THE PUZZLE IN FAMILIES

Treat each piece of information like it was evidence at a crime scene. I know that sounds really crazy but you will find it useful.

Purchase a cheap spiral notebook or record on your phone and begin your search by talking to your mom and dad. Ask them about their parents such as:

Birth Name, Birth dates and Locations where they were born. This can also be achieved by looking at your own birth certificate, it has your mother's maiden name and your father's birth name on it. It also has the location in which they were born. Granted, my grandmother tried to tell me about the family but as a child it went in one ear and out the other, now that I am much older, I wish I had listened to her.

The one thing that I remember the most; is on June 7, 1992, I saw my grandmother that morning as I went to my parents home to pick up my daughter. Speaking with my grandparents as I was leaving, my grandmother told me she wished I would do the family history and she would help me. What I didn't realize or expect was she would be deceased five hours later from a automobile accident. I could kick myself so many times over the years and then I smile when I think of how she would have loved to sit and talk about the family.

Some families don't mention family that lived outside their towns or counties. I don't understand it; but that is just a plain fact that you must deal with in your research. You will also have people tell you that they don't understand why anyone would wants to research the dead. It is simple to learn more about how I became who I am.

I'm outspoken and hardly meet a stranger, I take this trait from my grandmother, I can get a mean streak a mile wide, I soon learned that my great-grandmother had the same traits, so mix the two together and goodness, I'm doomed. My grandfather was quiet unless your misbehaved and goodness my butt would hurt.

I was told once that I have a heart of gold like my dad's mom, I never knew her but heard stories from her sisters that I look like her and act like her in some ways. They just didn't realize they were just encouraging my addiction to finding out my family history even more.

Each piece of information that you get about the people in your family is a clue.

So here are some things you must learn as a beginner that might help. Ask your parents if they have a copy of their birth certificates. If not, remember states were mandated in the early 1900's to begin recording the births and deaths. I found out that states and jurisdictions began keeping records at different times so calling the vital records department in the states you need to research help in determining if there is a birth certificate.

Birth certificates give the child's name, sex, birth date, and place of birth, name of the parents even the maiden name of the mother. The copy will cost about Twenty-Five Dollars.

If you can't find a record was filled out the time of the persons birth, then in some jurisdictions, they may have requested what is called a delayed registration of birth by showing proof of the birth as recorded in Bibles, School Records or even church records and testimony from a person that witnessed the birth. Delayed registrations did not become common in the United States until after 1937 when the Social Security Administration required proof of birth. The registration usually happened in the state in which the person was born.

A corrected record for the birth was filled sometimes if a name was changed, spelled incorrectly or added. Some cases required affidavits of eyewitnesses or evidence from other official records.

You can find a wide variety of records on the Family History Library sites but also on the Social Security Death Index which is all free. I found it was full of information, so use it freely.

(2.) The types of information on these certificates are valuable:
Child's Birth Name   Child's Gender
Names of parents and sometimes their ages at the time of birth.
Address of parents at the time of birth.
Date of Birth for Child
Maiden name of mother
Location of birth and sometimes the name of the hospital.
Parents birthplaces

Race of Child

Occupation of parents or parent

This also shows which children belong to what mother if there is multiple marriages and children.

(3.) Some people still actually keep birth, death and marriages in a family bible; it has become less over years with the digital world but there is nothing like holding the bible that your ancestors wrote in.

(4.) Church Records can be helpful but many are less common. If you know the church in which your ancestors went, write a letter to the church or call the Pastor to see if they have kept the records. I have found that the older churches have put their past records in books for people to look at.

(5.) Military Records or Military indexes are full of valuable information. Some sites provide free access to these digital records, some will require a paid membership. I've found it helpful to go to the Veteran Administration website and look for the form to fill out to just get the records from them if they are available. Some records were destroyed in a fire years ago and the government has been piecing together the files. It will take a few weeks but they do provide you with some records if they survived the fire. You must know the full name, social security number, unit and rank and which branch of the military they were in. This is just the cost of a stamp and waiting for the records. Confederate and Union Records can be found in many libraries microfilm, call the genealogy department of your town to see if they have these military records. You will find out a lot about your ancestors through these records and sometimes it has pension records included in these files. Libraries charge for copying but it depends on the library. I've been charged in some places ten cents up to fifty cents per page. I say it is well worth the copying and having these records in hand.

(6.)   Social Security Applications are full of helpful hints. The Record list the name at the time of death, birth, death date, mother and father. Ancestry has been the best in having these indexes and to look at the indexes could cost you. I recommend you get on the trial version for seven days and see what you can find in that amount of time if you like it join ancestry. I did this and spent a large amount of time writing down information on my ancestors. I choose to become a member after a couple of years and you have several different plans to subscribe to. Choose what works for you.

(7.)   A persons personal knowledge of the family history is worth a million bucks. Sit and talk to the person about what they remember growing up and ask if they remember family members. Even if they have just a first name it is a piece of the clue that could lead further. Ask about places, churches and who attended, some older folks might say they don't want to talk but they love spending time with visitors so it will be easy just to ask them simple questions about their family such as her or his mother and father.

NAME GAMES

THE OLD NAMING PROCESS

Generations in the past, naming a child contained members of their families. Some were named after family friends or famous people. This is the old English naming patterns.

I have found in doing research that a child was named for mothers, fathers, aunts, uncles, sisters or brothers.

Let me see if I can break this down for you in simple terms:

1st Son born was named after the father's father

2nd Son born was named after the mother's father

3rd Son born was named after the father

4th Son born was named after the father's eldest brother

5th Son born was named after the mother's eldest brother

1st Daughter born was named after the mother's mother

2nd Daughter born was named after the father's mother

3rd Daughter born was named after the mother

4th Daughter born was named after the mother's eldest sister

5th Daughter born was named after the father's eldest sister.

This was common if you look at the names of your grandparents, great-grandparents and all their children.

EXAMPLE:

Mary and John had five boys and three girls:

First child was a female named Louisa M.

(If the naming patterns were followed we have found the name of Mary's mother)

Second Child was a female named Martha

(Martha would be the name of the father's mother)

Third Child was a male named George

(George would be the name of the father's father)

Fourth Child was a male named James

(James would be named after the mother's father)

Fifth Child was a female named Mary

(Mary would have been named after the mother)

So you see within the names of the family you can find many common names. For example if Mary and Nancy were sisters, you will find common names within the families and so on within sibling families.

Sometimes you find the one name listed twice with different birth years.

It was not uncommon to name a child after a child that had died. I know it sounds weird but for example: John was born 1863 and

John L. was born in 1865. This tells me that either the first John born in 1863 has died or they just had a good name and stuck with it. Not being funny but I have seen this happen occasionally. I have seen families that really like a name and stuck with it, found in my odd family:

Benjamin U

Benjamin F

Benjamin W

These Benjamins went by their middle name and not their first names. You don't realize how many times I erased their names from my family tree because I thought I had made a mistake until they all appeared on the census together under the middle names:

B. Unsald

B. Floyd

B. Walker

The boys never went by their first names until it was put on the gravestones. So don't let names throw you off the trail. I have seen odd names out of the ordinary that will help in your search. It's been a hindering factor but sometimes a blessing with names.

The naming process died off somewhat about 1930 and people began using unique or unusual names. This makes it harder to trace because of not following the naming patterns. I think the naming pattern is a lost art; but we have kept the naming process in our family through the years and I am so glad my grandparents followed history of names.

When looking through records or files don't be thrown off by the spellings. I have found many different spellings for names. Example: Gearld= Gerld, Gerrie, Jerry, Jeri, Jerri, Jerl
John= Jon, Johnny, Johnnie, Jon Jon,

(8.)   You see it is more about looking beyond our ancestors dialect and the way others heard the name pronounced. I just kept a list in a notebook of how people have spelled a certain name.

Another thing to remember is when some ancestors came to this country, many family names underwent significant changes. The most common was in the spellings of names. Some emigrant ancestors deliberately changed their names to Americanized their foreign sounding names by shortening them or changing the spellings. Our ancestors did this in order to assimilate better and avoid discrimination that occurred by their cultural heritages. Some other changes took place by a persons spelling errors. People that kept the records in the United States or on ships passenger list may have accidentally misspelled the names due to not asking the correct spelling or dialect in which our ancestor spoke.

Some spelling changes are more dramatic and harder to recognize. The larger name changes happen over time, others happen all at once, particularly when a person moves from one place to another. A family may have several spellings of the same last name in the same location.

(9.)   When trying to determine if a name of different spelling is actually your surname, say it out loud instead of focusing on the letters themselves. Letters can be pronounced so many ways that I have had trouble making out correct names, it is only when I find several documents that give clues to the actual name spelling such as Bible records, Birth or Death Certificates, Marriage Records, Social Security Information or Military Records.

Some clues will become clear as ancestors used the mothers maiden name in some cases with children and some countries used different ways to use the naming patterns so it is easy to find information on the internet and books on different cultures in the naming process. It's worth using a couple of hours reading about the way different cultures names were used.

Another issue is nicknames, some can be difficult to catch if you happen to have the birth name but suddenly the census show a child you have not seen before. It is really straight forward such as: Katherine can be Kat, Kitty, Kit or Catherine can be: Cat, Cissy, Citty, Cate. Sometimes when you're new at genealogy it will make you look twice at information you have in your tree. A good idea would be to study common names used during your ancestors period of time.

NICKNAMES	GIVEN NAMES
Belle	Mable, Sybil

Bess, Bessie, Bettie	Elizabeth or Elisabeth
Betsy, Biddy, Beth	Elizabeth, Elisabeth
Bird, Birdie	Roberta, Alberta
Bob, Bobby	Robert
Bobbie	Barbara, Roberta
Carrie, Carry	Carolina, Caroline, Charlotte
Dick	Richard
Ed, Eddie, Eddy	Edgar, Edward, Edwin, Edwina, Edmond, Edmund

This is just a few names showing of how names can be shortened, you will get the hang of it after working on your family history for a while. It happens that people will appear on records and cemetery stones with their nickname instead of their birth names.

PICTURES

When I started my family history, my mother brought me a shoebox full of pictures. These had come from her parent's home, a few had names and years on the back but most didn't. After several days of going through these pictures, my mother and I had put names on ¼ of the pictures. Many are still unknown to me; but I keep going through them as I fill in my family history and I have discovered a few of the pictures in this box. It is still a work in progress and I hope one day I will have everyone named.

Ask your family for pictures of their families and children. Please ask them to put the names on the back and the year it was taken if they remember. Pictures mean so much when doing family history, you see the progression of the persons life through pictures.

Never use a ball point pen on the back of pictures as it leaves indention's into the pictures. I use a felt tip marker to write names and dates on back of pictures or labels placed on the back that have the written information on it for further reference. Digitalize all the photographs you get and put the originals you have in a safe locked place. Yes, I consider these valuable possessions. Never be shy about taking pictures at every event and document the people in the pictures to keep a record. It has been valuable to do this as many people doing memory Cd's have asked me if I had pictures of their loved ones. I gladly go through my pictures and pull any photographs I have for them and burn them on a disc or send them email to the person making the request.

(10.)   Many occasions, I have received pictures of my ancestors and have been told that by the person who shared it not to give it to anyone else. Well folks, I don't work that way. Once a picture is sent or given to me, it is my choice whom to share with. Some people think that keeping these pictures away from other family members is OK, but it is actually selfish but that is only my opinion. This is not to sway anyone of their choices but only to inform a person that family histories need to be shared. If we don't share the information we find, then it will get lost through the generations. I have made sure that my family history will be shared as I have created books for my family and their children.

When I visit a cemetery and it is not very large, I take pictures of every stone. This has been beneficial later when I discovered a new name and that person is buried in the same cemetery as other family members. I keep these pictures on jump drives and separate folders for quick reference.

When your searching, the best advice is to take pictures of ancestors headstones, also take pictures of the whole rows and five rows back and forth. This has paid off in great numbers. Some family members are buried close to each other and with the names changing of the females, you might find family within this line of taking pictures.

In keeping these different files of cemeteries, it became very helpful as I got further into my family history. This also prevented me from making return trips to the same cemetery. I have taken pictures of every stone in some large cemeteries as I was further away from home and didn't know when I would get a chance to return.

Every picture you take is helpful, but you can also use Find A Grave.com. This site is fantastic but remember that not every person has a stone and some don't have the picture of the stone. I am very thankful that many have put on Find A Grave obituaries, pictures and headstone pictures. It is a very useful tool to use in getting information on families. As I said before, if you use any of the information to reference the site or person in your family history.

Death Certificates
How useful are they?

Death certificates are a gold mine full of information. Listed below is some of the information you will find on a death certificate.

The county in which the death certificate was issued.

Deceased Full Name

Address of deceased

Race and Gender

Whether the person is married, divorced or widowed

Father's name and birth place

Mother's name including her maiden name and birth place

Occupation

Wife's name

Informant that gave information

Burial date and location

Funeral Home in charge

Cause of death

Date and Time of death

Sometimes on death certificates it has the parents birth location as unknown, this is because no one knows. In some cases it has the nickname of the person instead of their birth name. If Charles was his birth name but on the death certificate it has Charlie, it is easy to determine his birth name. If a birth name was Mary and on the death certificate it has Mollie, then this reverts back to the naming and nicknames that was already discussed in a previous section. After a while you can program yourself to know what nicknames are.

Don't become complacent when looking for death certificates on the internet. The downfall is not every state has these online but some have them up to certain dates. I gather what I can off the internet and make a list of death certificates that I need to order or go get. Ordering death certificates does cost money. I have been very fortunate that some people have already gotten the certificates and placed them on the internet for people to see.

I'm not saying every certificate provides all the information you might need but it does help. Many of my elder ancestors did not have the place of birth of their parents. If it did then I had a jump off point where to search, but take this with a grain of sand. Back in the early days people were told where they were born and found out later they were actually born in another state. People moved around back in the old days and sometimes places got mixed up.

Burial information is a great part of why I seek out death certificates. The location is important because I might find other family members buried in the same location. Since cremation is becoming popular; it is very beneficial to get a copy of an obituary if there is one or write to the funeral home to see if they would send you the information. I do this by either writing a letter, emailing or personally visiting the funeral homes. I have gotten so much information from funeral homes that launched my family search into all kinds of directions. I am grateful for those funeral homes that do help but don't be discouraged if they don't. Some funeral homes have policies that prevent them from giving you any information.

Something to remember for future reference, nicknames are used on death certificates and not the birth name. Examples: William might be listed as Bill, Mary might be listed as Polly, Robert might be listed as Bob. This is where I used the nicknaming sites that helped with these issues. This might seems confusing right now but it becomes very simple after a while.

When you look at a census record, the person taking the census information physically wrote down the information. Most Census takers never asked how to spell names and just wrote how they sounded; so you might find a variation of spellings for names and last names. Dialect was another issue that played a part in what the census taker heard when someone said their last name.

Check the birth certificate or death certificate against the last census you find the person on. At this time the Federal Census only goes to 1940 and not past that. The spelling of the names might be close enough to establish evidence that you have found the correct individual ancestor and or all of the family.

Looking through records such as death or birth certificates; you may discover the birthplace of the parents. Even looking at death certificate, under the informant box, this could give a clue to a relative such as father, mother, husband, sister. Not every certificate provides this information.

Burial: Most have the name of the cemetery in which the

ancestor is buried. Since cremation is becoming popular, it would be fruitful to seek out an obituary in the local paper, it sometimes gives the funeral home that provided the services for the deceased family.

I have emailed, written and even visited funeral homes to retrieve the information. Remember, not all funeral homes will corporate in your research. Don't take offense to this because some have policies that prevent them from helping; but some truly want to help and will.

Gravestones

The experience that I have accumulated over the years in searching cemeteries has proved to be enlightening.

A point to remember is to write information and photograph each stone you find of your ancestors.

I have found some stones of my ancestors that the birth and death dates that differ from any documented information that I have.

EXAMPLE: ED. BOWERS

BORN 1865

This example if from Juanita Bowers Owens ancestor, we discovered on the first census (Georgia 1900, Walker County) we found him on, listed his birth as 1864. The name is listed as Edmon or Edman and then on the next census (Georgia 1910, Walker County) the birth is listed as 1874. We also looked at the ages in which the person told the census taker. The last factor we took into consideration was on his gravestone it states 1865.

We now have three birth dates, but also we retrieved his death certificate and it states on it 1865. The informant on the death certificate was his father-in-law.

My friend is at a brick wall with her ancestor and the ED.; tells me that his name was either Edgar, Edmond or Edward. The shortening of the name or the use of a middle name has thrown our investigation off, but we will succeed.

Some stones have only the death year and some may have

complete information but this is up to whomever provided the stone maker with the information. Some people have put their marriage dates on the stones which is valuable information for any researcher.

Over the years, I have found the name of the spouse might be different on the stone and some of the reasons are jaw dropping: EXAMPLE:

Mary married Bill in the mid 1800's, between the census years, Bill dies and Mary remarries Robert, a man with the same last name. I found myself standing and staring at stones trying to figure this out until one day I had this light bulb go off in my head. Since I was new at genealogy and had no one to walk me through why this happening, I was stumped.

In the past, some females remarried a male within the family, maybe a brother, uncle and I have even seen a female marry her widowed father-in-law. Many males at that time felt the duty to take care of their brothers families if he died early.

You must remember in the early years, woman did not work and depended completely on the male to support her and the family, not like today's world. Researching in my early years, I admit I just went to take pictures of certain stones but I didn't see the bigger picture of my ancestors. My lesson in this section is take as many photographs as possible in a cemetery, it helps prevent return visits later on. As I have said before in most instances, family stayed close and some or all are buried close by.

My one lesson from going to graveyards was to take pictures of the every stone if it was not to large or take photographs for five rows forward and five rows backwards of the ancestor.

Headstones also teach many other things about ancestors, what clubs, organizations or military they might have served. Military stones are valuable in defining the time the person served his country.

Revolutionary War, War of 1812, Civil War, World World I, World War II, Korean War, Vietnam War, and any other wars or conflicts not mentioned.

Some military stones gives the positions, units, company, regiment and what branch they served. Another helpful hint, if a gravestone can't be read you can make it easier with limited resources. I was in on a research trip when I found several stones that were faded but you could feel the letters and numbers if your rubbed your fingers over it. I carry sidewalk chalk with me and rubbing it over the face of the stone can make the letters and numbers stand out, but use a bottle of water to wash the stone face after you do this. In a pinch, I have rubbed dirt over the letters revealing the numbers and letters; sometimes pouring water over the face of the stone also can reveal the writing on stones. ONE FACT: NEVER USE A PEN OR PERMAMENT MARKER ON ANY STONE.

MILITARY RECORDS

Looking at military records for ancestors can be a treasure troll of information.

- Some military records contain the full birth name of the individual.
- Birth state and even maybe the city where the person was born.
- Complete Birth dates, some have just the year.

Never be discouraged if the information on the birth year are missed by a couple of years. No birth certificates were issued until after 1900. The actual year dates that birth and death certificate were required to be kept by each state. Check with the State Vital Records Office to find out the year they began to keep these records. It varies from state to state.

Occupations might be listed on the military records and sometimes the employer. I have found some military records or military cards tell the name of relatives such as wife and children. Military records give descriptions of the individual whom is serving.

Many websites can be helpful, but reality is some ask for a membership fee. After several years of researching, I subscribed to Ancestry.com and have been a member for years. They have many records that can be accessed if you are a member. If you happen to have several people within your family working on family history, it is cost worthy to split the cost and use the same membership. To try many of the websites out that have a membership, do the trial version but make sure you make it clear the day before your trial version is over that you are discontinuing the trial version by sending an email or unsubscribing to the site. You might find some of these sites helpful, but in my experience many don't have all the records that I need so the cost is not worth it. The memberships depend on you and your budget.

FamilySearch.org is FREE. It is run by the LDS (Church of Latter Day Saints). I love this site but remember that it does sometimes refer you to sites that request memberships.

Fold3 request memberships for military records, Newspapers.com also another membership driven site that does not have every paper or article on it's site.

Many sites can provide a treasure of information for a researcher but the choice is up to you what you need to provide the best results.

Personal opinion is genealogy records should be free, but it is sometimes the best to bite the bullet and join one site.

I use a general search engine and type names in, some provide free information that someone has put on a website. Check out the family trees people have put on the net, some have posted, military records, marriage records, death and birth records, Bible records and even pictures.

Check out as many family trees, many have different information, some have posted pictures on their sites. Search for the states digital records, some states are beginning to put records on the net.

Helpful Sources

Rootsweb.com has many great resources, they will ask you to register but the site is free. Not all records are on this site but they do have information that might further your research.

Libraries can help if they have resources for genealogy. Many have expanded over the years to include a genealogy section. Copies for items will cost you.

Genweb.com is helpful in finding records such as marriages, death and census information.

Historical Societies are always full of information, many are more than willing to help in your search. Some family provide files for the historical societies and you can look through them. I have found a lot of information through others research. Remember to use those files as a guide. Mistakes can be made and it can throw your information off.

I have found fellow researchers files and snapped a picture of the page with my phone. Remember not ever place will let you use a camera but most will.

<u>WRITING TO PEOPLE</u>

IMPORTANT:

DON'T BE AFRAID TO WRITE PEOPLE.

Introduce yourself and how you are related to the person your are writing. Provide as much information you possibly can in your letter. Explain why you writing to the person or persons, provide as much detail as possible about your connecting relatives and ask politely if they have any information that might help your research.

This has served me well over the years. I have written and met so many new family members through writing. People have provided me with pictures, Bible records and I have been invited to so many reunions and still to this day, I keep in contact with all of them.

Funny thing is my distant cousins didn't know we existed and we didn't know anything about them. My family never talked about any family except the ones that lived close. Yet the cousins knew of us through the elders talking.

Most addresses can be found on the internet if you have the name, city and state in which they live.

REMEMBER: Not everyone will write back or talk to you, be sure to put your return address, phone number and email address in the contents of the letter.

You will not always get the quickest results when hunting a family member we call these BRICKWALLS.

This should never discourage you from researching your family.

It took many years for me to find several members of my family, don't dwell on it move to another ancestor. Sometimes clues will appear out of nowhere. I posted on family history forums and boards, searched other family members and have found names and locations where my hidden ancestors lived.

Take a genealogy DNA test, not ever DNA test will breakdown the roadblocks in your family history but it might provide names of other family members are blood related that could lead to getting through your brick wall.

If you become frustrated, put your family research away for a few days. I have done this on many occasions and suddenly realized that the clues I had read become so clear and I had the answers I was seeking.

I have visited so many government agencies getting records such as deeds, wills and marriage records but each courthouse charges different amounts for copies.

If you begin to fixate on one family member line, the opportunities for further information on the family will be missed.

I help many people with family searches for free and I get so frustrated when they don't want to expand their family search. I explain that researching other family members grows the knowledge of the family. If this is the direction that people want to research, I politely refrain from helping them.

I have been working on my family history since 1993, traveled thousands of miles both air and car, went through countless pages of deeds, wills and other records provided at courthouses. I have met so many people that I have great relationships with now that it is easier to get certain information that I need. This was the most enjoyable experience.

OBITUARIES

Whether you find obituary depends on if it was written up in the newspaper. Obituaries can be a treasure of information. Some have the person's full name, how old the person was at the time of death. In some cases and not everyone, the person's parentage is listed.

It will contain names of surviving family members, such as husband or wife, children (some cases a childs spouse) and grandchildren.

Also an important point to remember is to look at the pallbearers. In most cases it will contain family members names and friends.

This will help build your family history names. In recent years, some people have choose not to provide the newspapers with an obituary due to the cost that the funeral homes charge or the newspapers charge. I have seen them charged up to One Hundred Dollars per newspaper for a family to put in the paper. An alternative is to wait and provide the newspapers with your own obituary along with a death certificate. This is usually free. My personal opinion is it is a profit scheme of the funeral homes in a persons time of sorrow.

STRAIGHT FORWARD OR EXPANDED
FAMILY RESEARCH

Some people want to search the lines such as only father and mother but not siblings related to them.

This is fine; but many miss the big picture of their family history. I don't knock people for straight lining their family history; but if you do expand, trust me you will get more information that you think.

Expand your research to include sisters, brother, aunts, uncles and other relatives. The benefits is you learn so much more about the families in following all of your relatives.

I have read so many books on researching your family history. Some have valuable information, some are confusing and repeat information. Not many even mention cost of memberships or copying. I want to give you personal experience on researching and things that could help you.

Check out the free family history sites, some will help and guide you but some will cost you. I have spent thousands of dollars traveling, flights, copying, gas, hotels. It was well worth every penny I spent.

LOOKING AT OTHERS RESEARCH

Family trees on the internet or from files provided by other researchers should always be taken with caution.

Yes, they work hard on their information but not everyone researches but copies from others. Mistakes happen in names, dates, births, children and you should do your own research to ensure the information is correct.

Some researchers that put information on the internet change dates and other information. I don't put everything I have on the internet but when I find conflicting information, I proceed with caution.

Sometimes this helps in filling in the blanks but do your own research. I find mistakes or should I say differences of opinions but I never put down others for their research. Dates might vary, the number of children might be off, spelling errors happen but use the information as a guide. As your research expands so will your grasp of names, dates and information.

I usually find another avenue to travel in the family history from others but I am so thankful for their research. I admit I make mistakes all the time but I use the information that I have to guide me or I just leave blank until I can fill it later on.

Look for stories, diaries and pictures, use the history of the area to provide an insight into the landscape and the way people lived in certain times. I don't usually put every story on the internet because we are trying to research or should I say investigate the information.

Some people and this is a small percentage that don't want to share their information. That is their right but don't take offense to it. I have been very fortunate that people have been willing to share their information and resources. Always make a note in your comments or notes section of the person whom gave you the information.

I send a very short thank you note card to the individual that helped. You can purchase some thank you cards at discount stores. It is a personal way to thank a person for their help, I think it is very important to acknowledge your appreciation.

MARKS THAT PREVENT GOOD SEARCHES

I have noticed over the last few years that many people who put their family information on the internet have put certain flaws that prevent good searches.

"EXAMPLE"

,,Marvin Broyles,,NorthCarolina

or

OrangeCo.;NC

Another one that has shown lately is putting the state before the township or county. EXAMPLE: North Carolina, Orange C., Little River or my favorite I have found, LittleRiver,NorthCar*River. This is just a useless way to put in family history information. This is a perfectly example that will cause people to miss family members. Now look at the first example, putting commas in front of the names makes the search engines hunt the commas first. The second example makes a search engine search for OrangeCo.,NC as one word. Search engines do not separate words. In the first example it is looking for ,,Marvin. It is very important that you provide accurate spelling, spacing of names, places or states. This will help in faster searches and results.

Some people do this on purpose and some by accident. I have been working on cleaning up my family tree with correcting these errors. It is hard sometimes; but I use one hour a weekend to work on cleaning up mistakes, errors, correcting spellings. It has improved the amount of information that I have received from people. Please make sure you spell out everything, such as this example:

Orange County, North Carolina

or

Little River, Orange County, North Carolina

The more information you can correctly provide the search engine, the better your family tree looks.

As I wrote earlier, finding a search engine you like for your searches, a hint that helps is putting certain items in quotations. Example:

"George Taylor"

After I check out the results, I widen the search a little bit more by

"George Taylor" 1869

This gives the date and name to look for. The more you widen the search the list of criteria to certain things expands the search.

I guess most are familiar with the internet but with shrinking or expanding a search might help in your search.

CENSUS RECORDS

Many census records can be found on Ancestry.com if you are member. The 1890 census records were damaged or burnt in a fire and it leaves many people only to guess what people lived or died during that portion of time. I try to look for records provided by the counties during that period of 1890 to 1900. I found some states took their own census every five years but not many did this. It helped in finding if ancestors were living in the same place between the Federal Census.

You will find names, some birth dates, ages, male or female, relationship to head of house. It also can provide the years the parents have been married, how many children living and dead the mother had. It provides information about occupations, can they read or write, was anyone a veteran of a war. It takes time to go through these records but trust me it provides so much information. If a child is missing check five pages forward and five pages backwards. Some children married and started families of their own, so you might find them close by.

I have spent hours going through counties and counties of census records. I have found family members that moved to other close counties which only might be a few miles from the parents home. I never hurts to search other counties close to you ancestor.

HAND WRITING

As you work on your family history and dwell deep into wills, marriages and census records; you learn to read the hand written documents.

It's easy to read the different style types after a while. At first you will have some trouble but my suggestion is to look at names with the same letters. I have sat and examined names, checking out the F's and S's. It is a good idea to research hand writing of documents. Some wrote with the most beautiful hand writing and some swirled their letters together. It takes some studying on these documents but you will get the hang of it.

If you can't determine what a letter is, sometimes enlarging the document script helps.

No matter how many names, dates or other information you put into your family tree, it will never be completed. There is always marriages, births, deaths and other events you might want to memorialize in your family history.

Soon you will be able to grasp the huge amount of information that you receive. Sometimes it may overwhelm you, sometimes you think it is not enough. I tell people that I enjoying shaking the skeletons out of the closets, but some wish I wouldn't. I have learned to ask questions, never give up, never let a set back slow you down.

It is better to keep genealogy fun, exciting and to involve your children and friends. I wish everyone good luck on their quest. I hope you have the most successful time in searching your ancestors.

Kaye Edmondson Nicholson
Juanita Bowers Owens

www.ingramcontent.com/pod-product-compliance
Lightning Source LLC
Chambersburg PA
CBHW081757280526
45789CB00008B/2886